Resource Guide for Towing Industry Support Specialists

Preparation Material for the
Towing & Recovery Support Certification Program®
(TRSCP®) Advanced Level Exam

By Towing and Recovery Association of America, Inc.®
(TRAA)

Acknowledgments

The Towing & Recovery Support Certification Program® (TRSCP®) was developed from 2017-2018 with the support and grant funding of the U.S. Department of Transportation's Federal Highway Administration (FHWA). The TRSCP® is the first program of its kind within the incident management community.

The Towing and Recovery Association of America, Inc.® expresses its gratitude to the Women of the Towing & Recovery Association of America (WTRAA) for sharing their concept, FHWA for their continued support, and the dedicated professionals within the towing and recovery industry who served on the TRSCP® Advisory Committee. Without their time, energy, and expertise the TRSCP® would still just be an idea. Thank you on behalf of the entire industry and the professionals this program is intended to service.

<u>TRSCP® Advisory Committee</u>

John Borowski, Committee Member

Byron Harris, Committee Member

Kyle Herring, Committee Member

Cynthia Martineau, Committee Advisor

Elizabeth Martineau-Dupuis, Committee Chair

Lee Roberts, Committee Member

Gay Rochester, Committee Member

Geri Roskopf, Committee Member

Background

TRAA is publishing this guide as a resource for those working in the towing and recovery industry who are not themselves towing operators. Additionally, this guide may be used a study guide to prepare for the TRSCP® Advanced Level certification exam.

As a professional certification program, the Towing & Recovery Support Certification Program® (TRSCP®) is intended to measure certain basic knowledge, skills, and competencies that have been deemed appropriate for those employed in support staff roles within the towing and recovery industry. These roles include dispatchers, office managers, administrative staff, etc. Participants must demonstrate that they meet these predetermined standards by successfully completing the corresponding assessment with a final score of 75% or higher. Certification evaluates knowledge but does not address or attempt to evaluate the participant's actual job performance.

The Towing & Recovery Support Certification Program® (TRSCP®) is owned by, the intellectual property of, and its materials under Copyright by the Towing and Recovery Association of America, Inc.® (TRAA). As such, none of its materials or likeness may be used without the written permission of TRAA. This guide is intended for educational purposes only.

Contents

1. Introduction _____ 7

2. On-Scene _____ 9

   2.1 Equipment and Recovery Types...9

   2.2 Minor 11

   2.3 Intermediate 12

   2.4 Major...12

   2.5 Incident Action Plan...13

   2.6 Safety...15

   2.7 Documentation 16

   2.8 Social Media...17

3. Off-Scene _____ 19

   3.1 Customer Service...19

   3.2 Communication with the Right Agent(s) 20

   3.3 Post Incident Stages 22

   3.4 Company Safety Manager 24

   3.5 Post Incident Report 25

   3.6 Towing Traffic Incident Reporting System (TTIRS) 26

   3.7 Educational Opportunities 26

4. Glossary _____ 30

5. References _____ 31

6. About the Author _____ 32

1. Introduction

It is estimated that traffic incidents account for more than half of the traffic congestion in urban areas across the United States. The safe, quick, and effective clearance of traffic saves time, money, and the lives of motorists and responders. The major disciplines in Traffic Incident Management (TIM) are law enforcement, fire and rescue, emergency medical services, transportation, and towing and recovery professionals. Towing and recovery professionals are one of the only private sector partners on the TIM team. Visit the TIM website for more information: https://ops.fhwa.dot.gov/eto_tim_pse/about/tim.htm.

For towing and recovery professionals to effectively do their jobs, they rely on other industry professionals serving in supportive roles who are not themselves tow operators. While many don't work directly on the roadways, support personnel such as dispatchers, scene safety supervisors, compliance directors, and office managers are an integral part of the towing and recovery team. Agencies across the country recognize the need for trained and certified professionals to efficiently practice Incident Management (IM) and clear incidents in a timely manner.

The Towing & Recovery Support Certification Program® (TRSCP®) was developed as a national certification for individuals that provide support to incident management efforts but are not themselves tow truck operators. The entry level covered the basic competencies deemed necessary for someone working in a support role such as a dispatcher, office manager, or general administrative position. In this advanced level, we will expand on previously discussed topics and build on that knowledge base to introduce new topics specific to higher level support staff such as company safety managers, compliance directors, non-operator company owners, etc.

While the TRSCP® was developed specifically for the towing and recovery industry, the program is open to all qualified candidates in other associated fields that meet the requirements. If you are an agency dispatcher in law enforcement, 911, TIM, Department of Transportation (DOT), etc. we hope this program will enhance your understanding of the equipment, resources, and logistics necessary for an efficient towing and recovery response and, thereby, increase interdisciplinary communication. If you are a non-agency party that may be present at an incident scene (such as Public Information Officers (PIO), media, fleet safety directors, and insurance adjusters), we hope this will expand your knowledge base of incident management and quick clearance.

Regardless of the specific role, we hope that reading the study guide and passing the corresponding certification exam will fill you with a sense of accomplishment and confidence in the important part you play in improving the efficiency of incident clearance, decreasing roadway congestion, and increasing safety for both responders and the motoring public.

2. On-Scene

2.1 Equipment and Recovery Types

As a support professional working in an advanced role, your knowledge of equipment and recovery types will be paramount in assisting the towing operator and other incident management (IM) partners. Going beyond what we have already covered in the entry level, we're going to review additional equipment that towing and recovery professionals use and overview the general types of recoveries. This knowledge will help you in expediting decisions, such as which equipment to send, and earn respect with your IM partners.

Below is an abbreviated list of items and equipment that may be involved in a recovery. Every recovery is different, and recoveries can often be safely achieved by multiple means. For these reasons, we recommend talking with your tow operator(s) about the equipment they use frequently. Additional equipment that may be utilized during a recovery includes:

- **Snatch Block**- is a pulley block with a side plate that swings open. Because the side plate opens, you don't have to thread your winch cable through the opening; instead, you open the side plate, fit the cable over the pulley, and then close the side plate. A snatch block has two primary functions in recovery winching. The first is to change the direction of your winch cable when the anchor point is offset. The second is to increase the pulling power of your winch.

- **Scotch Blocks or Chocks**: are wedges of sturdy material placed closely against a vehicle's wheels and is typically attached by a chain to the tow truck's body to prevent movement. Scotch Blocks are placed for safety, in addition to setting the brakes, when winching. Scotch blocks are typically found on older tow trucks.

- **Hydraulic Rear Spades**- similar to scotch blocks, a hydraulic spade is permanently attached to the tow truck and uses hydraulic cylinders to raise and lower. They're used with parking brakes to help prevent movement when winching.

- **Outriggers/Stabilizer**- Stabilizers and outriggers have many configurations depending on the application and are used to minimize the risk of toppling when the center of gravity of the combined load and vehicle is outside the support base of the vehicle. Outriggers lift the vehicle's wheels off the ground while stabilizers do not.

- **Hook**- a piece of metal or other material, curved or bent back at an angle, for catching hold of or hanging things on.

- **Chain**- a connected flexible series of metal links used for fastening or securing objects and pulling or supporting loads. Chains are also used for fastening or securement.

- **Synthetic Rope and Web Slings**- The most commonly used synthetic web slings are made of nylon, polypropylene, and polyester. They also are the best choice for use on expensive loads, highly finished parts, fragile parts, and delicate equipment.

- **Wire Rope/Winch Cable**- is composed of individual wires that have been twisted to form strands. Strands are then twisted to form a wire rope. When wire rope has a fiber core, it is usually more flexible but is less resistant to environmental damage.

- **Air Brake System**- air brakes, or compression braking systems, use air pushing on a piston to apply pressure to a brake pad and stop the vehicle. Air brakes are common in large, heavy vehicles. Standard air-brake systems can be activated by pulling a button on the dash. Before you can drive a vehicle with air brakes, you must push in the emergency brake button to fill the system with air. As long as the emergency system is pressurized, the emergency brake will remain free. If the system has a leak, the pressure can decrease enough to engage the emergency brake.

- **Tow Truck Air Systems**- tow trucks are manufactured with fittings on the rear of the truck to supply air to the disabled vehicle to release the emergency brake system. Hoses and fittings are used to connect the disabled vehicle to the tow truck air system.

It is important to understand that many types of equipment have what is called a **working load limit** (WLL). According to the National Driver Certification Program®, the working load limit, "is the weight or load that equipment (allowing reasonable wear and tear) can safely bear under normal operating conditions"[1]. Using the equipment outside of these parameters can damage the equipment and pose serious safety risks to responders and the motoring public passing by the scene. Of course, equipment failure due to working outside the load limits also creates a longer recovery time.

Recovery types can vary widely based on the severity or classification of the incident. While every recovery is different, each type will generally require certain types of equipment. Understanding these wide-ranging categories will allow you to dispatch the correct equipment and better assist the tow operator. The general types of recovery categories are:

2.2 Minor

In general, a minor recovery could be defined as loading and towing an impacted vehicle at the scene without additional winching or recovery from off the roadway. Note, the impact scene could require minimal clearing of debris and absorbent material for minor non-HAZMAT fluid spills.

Equipment should be dispatched based on the vehicle's type, size, weight, and damage. Towing equipment utilized could be a flatbed, wheel lift, or under reach (also called an underlift). If

---

[1] (Towing and Recovery Association of America, Inc., 2004)

a trailer is involved, special equipment may be required for towing and transport such as a fifth wheel hitch, gooseneck hitch, or ball hitch. Vehicles with locked wheels or no keys may require dollies or skates.

2.3 Intermediate

An intermediate tow may require minor winching or recovery onto the roadway where it can then be prepared, loaded, and towed to its destination. Examples would include:

- A vehicle is upright, slightly off-road, and accessible with standard winch lines.

- The vehicle could also be stuck on some type of fixed object and may need to be lifted off the object before loading.

- The impacted vehicle could be missing wheels or have loose, corrupted vehicle parts that will need to be secured prior to the tow. Note, a larger debris field or vehicle spill will require additional time to mitigate.

2.4 Major

A major recovery will have the widest variety of conditions and require a detailed Incident Action Plan (IAP) to produce a safe, expedited clearing. These incidents can include vehicles:

- Overturned

- Extended distance off the roadway

- Extensively burned

- Entangled in high tension cables or guardrail median barriers

- Corrupted axles

- Heavy damage to the vehicle's body components

- Dispersed cargo

- HAZMAT commodities

- High quantity fluid spills

- Widespread debris field

Note, incidents involving multiple vehicles, fatalities, agency-controlled cargos, and specialized vehicles (such as cranes) can also fall into the major recovery category.

Major recoveries require the coordination of multiple parties. The IAP will determine what equipment and resources are required on-scene. While the prevailing conditions will ultimately determine the response, some basic elements to consider include:

- Recovery unit(s) for the class of vehicle involved

- Equipment or resources to recover cargo or handle disposal

- Transport unit or refuse containers for cargo

- Flatbed/trailer for debris removal

- Service truck

- Spill mitigation resource

- All terrain loader or other off-road equipment

- Specialized trailer transport unit

- Additional personnel

2.5 Incident Action Plan

An **Incident Action Plan (IAP)** is essential for an efficient incident clearance and responder safety. The IAP is the step by step roadmap for the recovery team to follow. Working together with all partners on-scene, the goal of the IAP is to identify tactical objectives, how to complete them, and the resources required[2]. After each objective is identified, the corresponding IM partner is allotted a designated amount of time to accomplish the task and keep the recovery progressing. Once implemented, the Command Staff will meet regularly to ensure that the targets are being met and make any necessary adjustments. These meetings are often referred to as **on-going size-ups**. If the scene changes or the recovery plan is modified, not uncommon in intermediate or major incidents, all IM partners need to be notified through the Incident Command System (ICS).

The IAP should encompass the entire scope of the recovery process including:

- Overview of scene including the location and condition of impacted units

- Equipment and personnel required

- Response activities by discipline

- Plans for dismissal of equipment and personnel

- Safety Concerns

    o Temporary Traffic Control & Traffic Monitoring

    o Hazardous Materials & Potential Hazards

- Any unusual factors present on-scene

- If cargo is present, does it require agency oversight?

- Post Incident Assessment

By working together in a coordinated effort, the recovery is more efficient and the scene is safer for both responders and the motoring public.

---

[2] (Federal Highway Administration, 2014)

2.6 Safety

Safety is a primary concern during an incident recovery. According to the Federal Highway Administration (FHWA) on-scene responders are struck and killed annually at the rate of twelve (12) law enforcement, five (5) fire and rescue, sixty (60) towing and recovery, and several transportation professionals[3]. That's an annual average of seventy-seven (77) people or more who don't make it home to their families and friends.

As an on-scene support staff you will play a key role in identifying potential safety concerns. For this reason, it is important to familiarize yourself with some of the conditions that can reduce scene safety and delay the recovery. Such conditions include:

- Equipment problems- cables and chains can break, truck malfunctions (broken winches, engine problems, etc.)

- Traffic flow (heavy rush hour traffic, etc.)

- Congestion at the scene

- Potentially unstable, hostile, or violent customers on-scene

- Cargo or hazardous materials

If you identify any areas of concern, report them to the IC Safety Officer (if applicable). As you may recall from the TRSCP® Entry Level, "the **Safety Officer** is responsible for monitoring on-scene operations and advising the IC on matters related to the safety and health of responders"[4]. Their tasks include:

- Identify hazards on-scene- One of the first actions the Safety Officer will perform is a walk-around to locate and identify potential hazards. Special attention should be given in lowlight

---

[3] (Federal Highway Administration, 2014)
[4] (Federal Emergency Management Agency, 2012)

environments, near utilities, and power lines. The Safety Officer will also be looking for any cargo present on-scene and the potential for hazardous materials.

- Participate in ICS meetings and review the IAP for potential safety concerns.

- Monitor the scene for potential safety concerns and exercise emergency stop authority if needed.

- Maintain a log of units and personnel on-scene.

The Safety Officer will also communicate with the ICS on-scene and designated parties off-scene. Their ability to properly maintain and relate current conditions at the scene is critical to a successful recovery. Without this vital function the scene can become chaotic and disorganized.

2.7 Documentation

When an incident occurs, it is always important to properly document the event. Thorough documentation of an incident creates a seamless transition between those on-scene and off-scene such as company management, vehicle owners, insurance companies, etc. Those off-scene need to have a clear picture of the incident and recovery even though they are not present on-scene. Proper documentation is especially important for customer service post incident and accurate billing.

Proper scene documentation begins at dispatching. As you may recall from the TRSCP®™ Entry Level, you'll need to gather and record a variety of information on each incident including:

- Time of notification

- The caller and/or vehicle owner's contact information including name, number, and insurance information (if applicable)

- Incident location including lane of traffic and number of lanes blocked

- Vehicle description including year, make, model, color, and plate number (if available)

- Reason for the call- collision, roll-over, service call, etc.

- Resources required- both equipment and personnel and a time log for each

- Incident severity- casualties involved and any other emergency response units on-scene (if applicable)

- Photo documentation of the scene- pictures of the incident, including various angles of the damage and location, allow for an accurate assessment of the scene as the incident moves through the remainder of its life cycle. Photo documentation is also invaluable for recording crash scene evidence/debris for crash reconstruction. Thorough and accurate scene photography can also provide a measure of liability insurance for operators on-scene.

Note, you should always check with your company to confirm your local and state documentation requirements and any applicable company policies. We recommend periodically reviewing these items in more detail in the TRSCP®™ Entry Level Study Guide.

2.8 Social Media

Many employees are proud of their work and recoveries are often unique and exciting. However, it is never appropriate or ethical to post pictures taken during a recovery to social media platforms, blogs, or websites without the written consent of the parties involved. The sharing of any accident information through the posting of scene photography or other methods may violate the policies of those involved and/or breach a private individual's privacy. We recommend every company set a clear and concise **social media policy** for their employees.

When posting work-related content online, employees must clearly indicate that their post is personal and of their own opinion. Content pertaining to sensitive company information should never be shared with the outside online community. Divulging information such as customer and/or vehicle information, internal company communications, internal operations, airing disagreements with fellow employees, and discussions of legal matters are strictly prohibited.

It is not uncommon for customers to use social media to air their grievances or file complaints. Employees should be asked to refrain from commenting or responding to a work-related matter unless they are an approved spokesperson using an official company account.

Employees are asked to remember that if they connect themselves with their employer's social media accounts their own personal posts will likely become visible to customers. This includes checking-in, tagging, and mentions. Even with the best intentions, the simplest post can harm the reputation of a company or the reputation of a customer. Before posting work-related material, everyone should take a moment to think about how someone may interpret the post. Always remember that a picture is worth a thousand words. Despite a worthy explanation in the caption or good-humored intentions, the public could assume an unintended message.

3. Off-Scene

3.1 Customer Service

Customer service is a key component to any towing and recovery business. As you may recall from the TRSCP®™ Entry Level, there are a variety of best practices for dealing with both internal and external customers. However, even in the best of circumstances customers will sometimes have complaints and he/she may be escalated to you depending on your position.

While handling an angry customer or complaint can be time consuming and unpleasant, there is always something to be learned from the experience. How you respond can make the difference between a customer who feels satisfied with the resolution and one who vows to never patronize your business again. It's not always about being right, it's about always being willing to make it right.

- **Listen**- Often times, mistakes will occur because we didn't listen and gather the correct information needed. Taking the time to fully listen to a customer and remaining calm, helps a customer gain trust and confidence in you. Maintain eye contact if the customer is in front of you and give them your full attention.

- **Acknowledge**- Recognize where the person is coming from (even if you don't agree with them). If you or the company has done something wrong, apologize openly.

- **Resolve**- What can be done to reach an amicable solution? Clearly explain which options are available. Once an option has been agreed upon, see it to completion and don't make promises you cannot keep.

- **Thank**- Extend your gratitude to the person for being a customer (even if it wasn't by choice). Showing appreciation for them, their business, and their willingness to find a resolution will give you the best likelihood they'll leave the interaction with a positive impression.

Each and every customer complaint should be taken seriously. To ensure the best possible customer service, and protect the interests of the business, we recommend establishing a written policy for customer complaints. As an employee, it is important to familiarize yourself with this policy if applicable. Depending on your position, you may be the one escalating a customer to your manager or you may be the one receiving the customer being escalated.

3.2 Communication with the Right Agent(s)

One of the most challenging issues during and after a recovery can be ascertaining the correct contact information for the vehicles' designated agent. Legally, it is imperative that you only communicate with the correct agents regarding a vehicle's status and outcome. Three common scenarios are:

- **Owner Occupied**- this is the easiest scenario. If the owner is with the vehicle, or was the one to contact you requesting services, you can get his or her contact information and insurance information (if applicable) directly from the source.

- **Owner unavailable or incapacitated**- If still on-scene, ask the investigating agency for the vehicle's owner and insurance information. This will be your most accurate, easily accessible resource. If the information is not available from the investigating agency, check the vehicle for registration and insurance documents (often found in the glove box). Note, some companies do not permit this. Please refer to your company's policy. If the information isn't available with the investigating agency or documentation in the car, the next option is to consider using outside resources that offer vehicle information data for a fee. This will be the best resource for passenger and non-commercial vehicles. If the vehicle has a commercial identifier number (DOT or IFTA number), you can check the FMCSA Safety and Fitness Electronic Records (SAFER) System or other USDOT weblinks for information on the registered carrier. Note, the data could be outdated if the reporting is delayed in the event of insurance change or vehicle sale. You can also perform a web search for a contact number based on the vehicle's markings. Make sure you have the full VIN of vehicles involved to correctly identify the ownership and insurance information.

- **Tractor trailers or trucks (with or without cargo)**- When a tractor trailer is recovered there could be four (4) or more parties involved. The ownership and insurance for the tractor, trailer, any load and its contents can make discussions complex to say the least. If the incident was the result of an outside party, then their ownership and insurance also become a variable. Often insurance companies try to separate responsibilities between the tractor and the trailer. Of course, the load or cargo will not be at fault and the sender or receiver will be interested in getting the load released immediately. Loads that may be in danger of contamination are especially complex. The presiding agency authority, based on jurisdiction and type of commodity, will often deem a load with perishable food products contaminated in its entirety. In these cases, provisions will be necessary for land fill and proper disposal causing additional charges.

The laws regarding communication and notification vary by state and municipality. Be sure to familiarize yourself with the laws and requirements in your area.

Once you have identified the appropriate agent you also have to ensure that you're communicating correctly. One person from your company should be designated as the point of contact for that customer, whether the vehicle owner, insurance company, or other third-party. Any and all parties need to receive the same clear and concise information. Customers may not know the process facing them and need to understand the options available to them.

3.3 Post Incident Stages

The work isn't done when the scene is cleared. There are a number of potential stages and outcomes for a disabled vehicle after the incident. Understanding these stages, and any related customer service needs, will assist you in your role.

As we covered in the TRSCP®™ Entry Level, the outcome of a vehicle is dependent on a number of factors including the extent of the damage and insurance[5]. The insurance company may determine that a bill is covered, they may try to negotiate your rates, or determine no liability on the insured's behalf. Ultimately the vehicle owner is the responsible party for any towing and storage charges. Insurance companies only have an obligation to the insured.

Historically, the legal system will not permit an endless storage bill. Process the vehicle in accordance with your state law. If the vehicle is totaled, abandoned, or otherwise becomes the possession of the company, it may end up being either salvaged or auctioned.

- **Salvage**

In the event that the tow company decides to obtain ownership of the vehicle, a current unbiased salvage value needs to be determined. This is typically done by obtaining several quotes/prices from different sources; i.e. Kelly Blue Book or similar, local used car dealers, and local classified ads to determine a realistic value. The salvage value amount is then credited to the outstanding invoice leaving either a balance due to the tow company or credit owed to the vehicle owner. Unless prohibited by state or local regulations, any outstanding monies owed can then be pursued through a legal process in the court system or collections. The next steps may vary based on the condition and value of the vehicle, it may be repairable, scrapped or move on to the auction

---

[5] (Towing and Recovery Association of America, 2018)

stage. Please refer to your state or local regulations as it pertains to this part of the process. Be sure to adhere to all notification requirements.

- **Auction**

In the event that the vehicle is a total loss, an auction would be the next step in the vehicle's life cycle. There are several options when it comes to the auction process. Auctions can be done online, public, or private. The auction process needs to be strictly adhered to and in full accordance with your state or local regulations for final disposal. Please refer to your state or local regulations as it pertains to this part of the process. As with the above salvage process, the final invoice is determined by adding all auction costs to the towing and recovery invoice and then deducting the auction value, leaving a final balance due or credit owed. Unless prohibited by state or local regulations, any outstanding monies owed can then be pursued through a legal process in the court system or collections.

At the end of a vehicle's life cycle, the vehicle's information will need to be submitted to the **National Motor Vehicle Title Information System (NMVTIS).** This "kills" the vehicles vehicle identification (VIN) number and prevents fraud and theft. It is important to understand that any entity that owns, controls, handles, acquires or sells five (5) or more junk or salvage vehicles per year (including vehicles declared a total loss) is required to report the vehicle information to NMVTIS through an approved third-party data consolidator[6]. Familiarize yourself with the NMVTIS reporting requirements to determine when your company is required to report and what vehicles are reportable. The U.S. Department of Justice's *Policy Clarification Regarding Tow Operators/Towing*

---

[6] (U.S. Department of Justice, 2011)

Companies Reporting Requirements clearly defines the process[7]. Remember to keep good records and document each stage of the vehicle's life cycle.

Note, these are general policies and practices. Always default to the specific laws, policies, and procedures in your area.

3.4 Company Safety Manager

Safety is a paramount concern for all incident responders. We've already covered a variety of safety concerns and best practices. Taking them one step further, we recommend that all companies servicing intermediate or major incidents designate a **company safety manager**.

The company safety manager's goal is the safety of all employees. The company safety manager may, or may not, be present on intermediate or major scenes depending on the established incident command system (ICS). Off-scene, they are responsible for several important safety tasks:

- Developing a written safety program for the company- A safety program manual needs to be developed covering all potential hazards within a company including on and offsite. Employees need to receive a copy of the written program and testify that they've read it thoroughly by providing their signature. Any employees not adhering to the program need to be notified and documented. Continual violators need to go through the disciplinary process including potential position reassignment or dismissal of employment.

- Host regular, mandated safety meetings- safety meetings need to include any incidents since the last meeting, any improvements, and any impending safety concerns.

---

[7] (U.S. Department of Justice, 2011)

- <u>Performing frequent site audits and equipment inspections</u>- regular inspections and audits of both the site and equipment need to be documented and filed for future use. Documentation should include a full dated explanation of all deficiencies and required remedies.

- <u>Provide and maintain safety and equipment education</u>- the company safety manager is responsible for ensuring that all new and ongoing employees are appropriately educated on all company safety policies and equipment. This can include both in-house and external educational programs. The company safety manager is responsible for ensuring the employee's trainings, certifications, licenses, etc. stay current and up-to-date.

3.5 Post Incident Report

The **post incident report** is extremely important to the overall success of a towing and recovery business. Post incident reports outline the incident so an invoice or bill can be generated for the customer. While you may not be the one generating the invoices in your company, you can support your colleagues by understanding the basic structure and content of these reports.

The post incident report is created using the information and documentation gathered throughout an incident. The report should include:

- Any available **photo** documentation.

- A **detailed synopsis** of the incident, including:
  - The volume and duration of resources on-scene including equipment and personnel (this data should already be recorded in the incident's time log).
  - Any special circumstances or hazards that may require special billing such as hazardous materials, etc.

- Any other pertinent details as required by your company's policy.

With the information outlined above, the billing department will be able to generate a complete and professional invoice for the customer. While billing and invoicing may be unpleasant, a clear and detailed invoice improves customer satisfaction and decreases the likelihood of complaints.

3.6 Towing Traffic Incident Reporting System (TTIRS)

Given the nature of the work, tow operators can sometimes find themselves in an unsafe work environment. Despite all the safety protocols, it is impossible to predict the actions of the motoring public and guarantee safety. While all states now have Move Over/Slow Down laws, they are not yet widely adhered to on our nation's roadways. We hope the enforcement of these laws will continue to improve for the benefit of all IM partners.

If a tow operator is involved in an on-scene roadway near miss, struck by, or fatality it is imperative that it be reported to the **Towing Traffic Incident Reporting System (TTIRS)**. The TTIRS was developed by the Statewide Towing Association, Inc. of Massachusetts as the nation's only reporting system for the towing industry[8]. The goal of the TTIRS is to collect and quantify this important safety data and make it available to state towing associations. The data is essential for supporting Move Over enforcement and developing procedures to make roadside work safer for the towing industry. Participation is voluntary and free for tow companies, operators, and government agencies to report incidents. To learn more or report an incident to the Towing Traffic Incident Reporting System, go to www.TTIRS.com.

3.7 Educational Opportunities

As a valued member of the towing and recovery team, it is important to understand the many educational opportunities available for both operators and support staff such as yourselves.

---

[8] (Towing Traffic Incident Reporting System, 2018)

Programs range from professional certification to training and cover a variety of towing and recovery and IM topics. Some courses will be specific to the industry while others include the wider IM team.

The **National Traffic Incident Management (TIM) Responder Training** is the most integrated IM program. It brings together team members from all the incident management disciplines with the goal of furthering communication, expediting roadway clearance, reducing traffic congestion, and increasing responder safety[9]. This important training is available both online and in-person. The online training is readily accessible on the National Highway Institute's website: https://www.nhi.fhwa.dot.gov/course-search?course_no=133126. A small number of programs have been deemed equivalent to the National Traffic Incident Management (TIM) Responder Training by FHWA.

The **National Driver Certification Program® (NDCP)** is the towing and recovery industry's only professional certification program. Developed in collaboration with the Department of Transportation's FHWA in 1995, the NDCP retains its distinction as the only industry program recognized by the organization[10]. The NDCP is designed as an independent, third-party evaluation of an operator's knowledge base. Due to the broad scope and lack of bias in professional certification, successfully passing a certification exam indicates that the operator has acquired the knowledge deemed necessary to perform the occupation[11]. The program includes Level 1- Light Duty, Level 2- Medium/Heavy Duty, and Level 3- Heavy Recovery Specialist®. Proctored certification exams are readily available online.

---

[9] (Federal Highway Administration, 2014)
[10] (Towing and Recovery Association of America, Inc., 2014)
[11] (Institute for Credentialing Excellence, n.d.)

While those options are geared towards the tow operator and on-scene responders, there are more programs that will prove invaluable to your work in a supportive role. Participating in cross-disciplinary training is essential to increasing your level of awareness and your ability to act quickly and make sound judgments in conjunction with other responding partners. The **National Incident Management System (NIMS)** provides a consistent national approach for Federal, State, and local governments, and the private sector to work together to prepare for, respond to, recover from, and mitigate domestic incidents, regardless of cause, size, or complexity[12]. Based upon emergency management and incident response practices, NIMS represents a core set of doctrine, concepts, principles, terminology, and organizational processes that enable effective, efficient, and collaborative incident management. The NIMS process is broken down into a series of easily digestible courses available both online and in-person. These courses are essential for anyone working within the incident command system or a leadership/supervisory role. Everyone involved in emergency management, regardless of discipline or role, should take the NIMS baseline curriculum courses (Independent Study-700 and ICS-100). These courses will provide a baseline for ICS and NIMS.

Another important educational opportunity lies in the field of HAZMAT response. Any vehicle involved in an incident, regardless of size or class, could potentially carry hazardous materials. The Occupational Safety and Health Administration (OSHA) provides several online courses that are vital for the safe and effective handling of HAZMAT scenarios. The **Emergency Management Institute's Introduction to Hazardous Materials** course (IS-5.a) is a good starting point[13]. All employees, on and off-scene should take this course.

---

[12] (Federal Emergency Management Agency, 2018)
[13] (Federal Emergency Management Agency, n.d.)

Unlike our IM partners, there is no set standard or curriculum for training within the towing and recovery industry currently. Training within the industry is typically done in-house or offered by outside, private companies and in some cases state organizations. Training opportunities vary from state to state and include everything from light to heavy duty. Upon completion of a training program the operator should receive a certificate of completion for the course. Note, a certificate of completion, or assessment-based certificate, is not equivalent to certification[14]. For information on specific training opportunities in your state, we recommend contacting your state towing association.

Educational requirements for towing operators vary by municipality, state, and type (private property, police ordered, etc.). Check regularly with your local authorities to confirm your unique requirements and be aware of any changes. It's always best to be on top of these requirements instead of getting caught off guard.

Ongoing education is important whether or not it is specifically required for your company. From a bottom-line perspective, employing the most qualified staff can be an advantage when applying for contracts and negotiating rates with insurance companies as those operators are less likely to be involved in a crash. Many companies also find that promoting the education of their drivers on their website, business cards, and other marketing materials helps drive business and differentiates their company from their competitors. Lastly, focusing on education improves employee morale and professionalism.

---

[14] (Institute for Credentialing Excellence, n.d.)

4. Glossary

Glossary Term	Description
Auction	Vehicle auctions are a method of selling salvage, used, repairable or new vehicles.
Incident Action Plan (IAP)	The IAP is a written plan that defines the incident objectives and reflects the tactics necessary to manage an incident during an operational period (FEMA Incident Action Planning Guide, 2012).
National Motor Vehicle Title Information System (NMVTIS)	The National Motor Vehicle Title Information System (NMVTIS) is designed to protect consumers from fraud and unsafe vehicles and to keep stolen vehicles from being resold. NMVTIS is also a tool that assists states and law enforcement in deterring and preventing title fraud and other crimes (National Motor Vehicle Title Information System, 2018).
Salvage	Salvage refers to a vehicle that has been deemed a total loss.
Towing Traffic Incident Reporting System (TTIRS)	The TTIRS was developed by the Statewide Towing Association, Inc. as the only national, online, voluntary, reporting system for the towing industry (Towing Traffic Incident Reporting System, 2018).
U.S. Department of Justice (DOJ)	The DOJ was created to enforce the law and defend the interests of the United States according to the law; to ensure public safety against threats foreign and domestic; to provide federal leadership in preventing and controlling crime; to seek just punishment for those guilty of unlawful behavior; and to ensure fair and impartial administration of justice for all Americans (About DOJ, 2018).
Working Load Limit (WLL)	The maximum load in lbs. that should ever be applied to a chain when it is new or in new condition. This rating applies only when the load is uniformly applied to a straight length chain (Towing and Recovery Association of America, Inc., 2004).

5. References

(2018, March). Retrieved from National Motor Vehicle Title Information System: https://www.vehiclehistory.gov/

About DOJ. (2018, March). Retrieved from U.S. Department of Justice: https://www.justice.gov/about

Federal Emergency Management Agency. (2012, October). *Position Qualifications for Operational Coordination: Incident Management.* Retrieved February 2018, from https://www.fema.gov/.../fema_509_2_safetyofficer_20130110_v.2.0_clean.pdf

Federal Emergency Management Agency. (2018, February). *National Incident Management System.* Retrieved February 2018, from https://www.fema.gov/national-incident-management-system

Federal Emergency Management Agency. (n.d.). *IS-5.A: An Introduction to Hazardous Materials.* Retrieved February 2018, from Emergency Management Institute: https://training.fema.gov/is/courseoverview.aspx?code=IS-5.a

Federal Highway Administration. (2014). National Traffic Incident Management (TIM) Responder Training. *4-Hour TIM Responder Training Course.* Washington, DC.

FEMA Incident Action Planning Guide. (2012, February). Retrieved from FEMA.gov: https://www.fema.gov/media-library-data/20130726-1822-25045-1815/incident_action_planning_guide_1_26_2012.pdf

Institute for Credentialing Excellence. (n.d.). *Certificate vs. Certification.* Retrieved February 2018, from http://www.credentialingexcellence.org/p/cm/ld/fid=4

Towing and Recovery Association of America, I. (2018). Towing & Recovery Support Certification Program Entry Level. Washington, DC.

Towing and Recovery Association of America, Inc. (2004). National Driver Certification Program Medium/Heavy Duty Study Guide. Washington, DC.

Towing and Recovery Association of America, Inc. (2014, February). *NDCP Certification.* Retrieved February 2018, from http://traaonline.com/certification/

Towing Traffic Incident Reporting System. (2018, May). Retrieved from Statewide Towing Association, Inc.: http://statewidetowing.org/towing-traffic-incident-report-system-ttirs/

U.S. Department of Justice. (2011). *Policy Clarification Regarding Tow Operators/Towing Companies Reporting Requirements to the National Motor Vehicle Title Information System (NMVTIS) Under the Anti Car Theft Acts.* Washington, DC. Retrieved from https://www.vehiclehistory.gov/Tow_120611.pdf

6. About the Author

The Towing and Recovery Association of America, Inc.® (TRAA) is the "The Voice of America's Towing Industry"! Founded in 1979 in Kansas City, Missouri TRAA is the umbrella trade group and national voice of the towing and recovery industry, which is estimated to include 35,000+ towing businesses in the United States. TRAA's membership includes professionals from the United States, Canada, and abroad.

TRAA is a 501 (c)(6) nonprofit membership national towing association, governed by a representative board of directors whose officers are elected from the membership.

TRAA represents the interests of the towing and recovery industry on Capitol Hill, sponsoring annual events and meetings that are attended by members as well as state association officers and leaders. TRAA also produces an array of educational products supporting professionalism in towing and recovery and in business management.

Made in United States
North Haven, CT
28 April 2024

51858046R00020